THUNDERFEET

ALASKA'S
DINOSAURS
AND
OTHER PREHISTORIC CRITTERS

By SHELLEY GILL   Illustrated by SHANNON CARTWRIGHT

THUNDERFEET

The story of Alaska's dinosaurs and other prehistoric critters

Manufactured in China by C&C Offset Printing Co.Ltd.Shenzhen, Guangdong Province in December 2018

Library of Congress Card Number 88-090797
ISBN 13: 978-093400-719-1 (pbk)
ISBN 0-934007-19-5 (pbk)
ISBN 0-934007-04-7 (hc)

PAWS IV
Published by Sasquatch Books
1904 Third Avenue, Suite 710
Seattle, Washington 98101
(206) 467-4300
SasquatchBooks.com

THUNDERFEET

is dedicated
to all of Alaska's animals.
We hope the Last Frontier will stay a wild place.

Alaska's biggest critters
roam this land no more.
All that's left are teeth and bones
of the Arctic dinosaur.

In the land where caribou now roam, there once lived strange and amazing creatures. Thousands of them moved across the hot land in dusty herds, stripping the plants and trees of leaves. Others hunted alone, stalking their prey in the murky fern forests. Alaska's dinosaurs romped and stomped their days away in the warm dawn of the Last Frontier.

Did Alaska's dinosaurs live in the dark?
  It's a prehistoric question mark.
Maybe they migrated like caribou,
  traveling south to rendezvous.
Were fallen leaves what they ate?
  Perhaps they had to hibernate.

Of course Alaska's dinosaurs are long gone now. We found out they once lived here when paleontologists discovered their bones in a riverbed on the North Slope. By studying plant fossils 70 million years old we know that it was much warmer then; about like southern Canada today. Winter days were short and the leaves fell from the trees each autumn. Do you wonder what the dinosaurs ate when the leaves were all gone? How did they survive during the months of darkness? Did they migrate south? Did they curl up like black bears and sleep all winter? Or did they go on a dinosaur diet?

A duck-billed creature named Hadrosaur
  munched on plants all day.
She built her nest on the forest floor
  and lined it with twigs and hay.
With a honk and a bellow she circled,
  protecting her precious eggs.
One by one they began to hatch,
  in a tangle of beaks and legs.

Hadrosaur
HAD-row-sore

Huge herds of hadrosaurs lived along a big delta that ended at the edge of an ancient Arctic sea. The soggy land was formed from silt dropping from the streams that bubbled down from the Brooks Range. The hadrosaur probably laid her eggs under the nearby sequoia trees. No bigger than a hotdog bun at birth, each baby would grow up to be about the size of a pick-up truck.

The quick and cunning Tröodon
slinks through damp and dew,
Stealing the eggs of hadrosaur,
swift, and sleek and shrewd.

Troodon was a crafty little dinosaur. Crouching close by, he would wait until the mother hadrosaur wandered away, then he quickly climbed into the nest and cracked open all the eggs. While he chewed on baby dinosaurs, he tested the air currents for the dangerous scent of some bigger carnivorous creature who might fancy a morsel of Troodon meat.

Tröodon
TROO-don

The Tyrannosaurus tyrant
   was a terrible lizard giant.
Born to rip and slash,
   through fern trees he would crash.
Hunting for his midday meal,
   or a snack that he could steal.

Tyrannosaurus
teh-RAN-o-sore-ruhs

Alaska's Tyrannosaurus was a small variety of the famous meat-eater. He ripped his food apart with razor sharp claws on his hind legs and his terrible teeth tore into any hapless hadrosaurs who fell behind the herd. But the tyrannosaurus may have depended on luck for many of his meals. He couldn't run very fast and his front legs were so short they were practically useless. If a hadrosaur knocked the tyrannosaurus over with a sharp smack of her tail, the tyrannosaurus probably had a tough time getting back on his big feet.

In this wilderness Alaska,
volcanoes hissed with steam.
Ceratops nibbled on horsetails
that lined the silty streams.
The suck and slurp of feeding
was the hadrosaur, not moose.
The wind bent fragile seedlings
of the cypress trees, not spruce.

Ceratops
SERR-uh-tahps

The fact that dinosaurs even lived in Alaska came as a big surprise to some folks. But paleontologists had a couple of good clues. After all, the coal beds and oil fields dotting the North Slope are just a lot of old squashed plants and ocean stuff left over from the dinosaur days. Now that actual bones and fossils have been found, there is a lot more work to be done.

Where did the dinosaurs come from?
Where did the dinosaurs go?
Did they disappear forever?
I guess we'll never know.

Dinosaurs ruled the world for millions of years. Then, quite suddenly, they were gone. Scientists still don't know what happened. It could have been a change in climate, a deadly disease, or even an asteroid from outer space. Whatever it was, it killed them all.

plesiosaur
PLEASE-ee-o-sawr

Now little critters
   soft and furry
peek from rocks,
   startle, then scurry.
Where are the thunderfeet
   who filled them with dread?
But that day is over;
   the dinosaurs are dead.

Once the dinosaurs were gone, the small, warm-blooded mammals could come out from hiding. It took a couple of million years, but eventually those few, early types of rat-like varmints became a zoo of amazing and wonderful critters. Some, like bats, took to the air. Others, like whales and sea lions, chose the sea. But most continued to live on dry land and because the land continued to change, so did the animals.

When two drifting pieces
of earth collide,
one goes low;
one goes high.
Smashed together,
the land takes form.
That's how the mountains
in Alaska were born.

Land bridge

Asia

Mantle

Mount Denali was reaching for the sky when it began to get so cold in the Arctic that most of the water froze in great sheets of ice. The oceans became shallow and in the west a bridge of land was left high and dry. This was not Alaska's first ice age and it would not be the last. As the land began to freeze and dry out, a whole parade of critters migrated from Asia onto the broad grassy plain that was interior Alaska. Later, when the climate warmed again and the ice blanketing North America melted, another group of animals would travel here from South and Central America.

Ocean crust

Alaska

The mastodon
   was a mega-mammal,
like the stupendous sloth
   and the colossal camel.
But beg your pardon,
   one beat them all;
the short-faced bear
   was ten feet tall.

As the land and climate changed, Alaska's animals grew long hair and thick fur to protect themselves from the colder weather. In fact, they GREW, period. Big horses, stag moose, mastodon, and bison lost less body heat because of their size. The giant short-faced bear was about the size of a Kodiak bear, but he had short stubby claws and a short stubby snout. His legs were long, though, and he may have been one of the best hunters in history.

What made you get so shaggy?
 Why are your tusks so long?
How come your knees are baggy?
 Were mammoths all this strong?
And what about those yak-itty yaks?
 What kind of cows are these,
with floppy ears and hairy backs
 and horns the size of trees?

Summers were hotter and winters were colder as the bitter winds scoured the steppes. Nights were clear and, during the summer, wildfires burned out of control, charring the land and leaving beautiful sunsets blazing in the western sky.

The buff-colored pony
  was very wary
as she nibbled on stalks
  and ripened berries.
A lion scent
  rode the air,
haunting and taunting
  the wild red mare.

Crouching in the rocks and the tall grass, the meat-eaters stalked the grass-eaters. The cunning sabre-toothed cat used her two fangs like a set of wicked knives, ambushing the steppe pony and saiga antelope. The cat killed by tipping her prey over and ripping open their soft bellies.

Wolves and moose and caribou
wander under skies of blue.
As camels crunch the frozen hay,
musk-ox sleep the day away.

Some of the creatures who shared the plains with the mammoths and lions still live on the tundra today. Wolves have been chasing caribou for a long, long time. Moose and musk-ox search for the tender willow shoots early each spring. The dragonfly still hovers over ponds in the summer, but critters like the mammoth and the sabre-toothed cat eventually disappeared, just like the dinosaurs did.

The sparkle on the glacier
is melting snow and ice.
The grass has gone to tundra.
No mammoths now, just mice.

Of course, unlike the dinosaurs, the mammoth mystery may have been solved. Warm weather caused the ice sheets to melt and the land bridge sank under the sea. In this new warmth, bushes and finally trees began to creep north, replacing the lush grasses on the steppe. Animals who could change their diet to include these new plants survived. But grass-eaters like the mammoth and the yak starved.

Dragonflies still remember
Alaska in her birth.
They were perched upon the horsetails
when dinosaurs ruled the earth.
Floating on the north wind
they heard the mammoth's call.
Alaska keeps on changing
and they've been here for it all.

Ask an old-timer, or a dragonfly, if the weather is different now than it was twenty years ago and they'll tell you it is a lot warmer than it was in the "old days." Glaciers are melting, ferns grow tall at the edge of the spruce forests and horsetails still line the streams that flow from the Brooks Range. Who knows what will happen in the next million years?

Maybe, just maybe, the dinosaurs aren't done with Alaska yet.

GLOSSARY

Fossil - remains and traces of earlier creatures and plants encased in mud or rock. In Alaska scientists found dinosaur fossils of tyrannosaurus, ceratops, tróodon and hadrosaur.

Paleontologist - a student of prehistoric life.

Extinction - There have been several mass extinctions during earth's history. Some scientists say asteroids, comets or a supernova caused a sudden extinction when earth's atmosphere was plunged into darkness, killing plant and dinosaur alike. But Alaska's fossil find may prove to be very important, because our dinosaurs faced the threat of cold and darkness regularly each winter. Learning more about how this group might have lived under such harsh conditions could help solve the puzzle of the dinosaur's death.

Plants - The horsetails, cypress, ferns and sequoias of the dinosaur days were quite simple compared to all the lush greenery on earth today. It took millions of years before the first flower bloomed and the first berry fell . . .

Plate tectonics - the theory that the earth's surface is made up of moving plates that float like ships on a molten sea of hot rock. The continents ride plates that collide with each other as they drift along. When one plate crashes against another, a mountain range may rise and rumple much as a rug does when you push it into a corner. When the ocean floor collides with the edge of a continent it plunges back into the earth's interior, forming an ocean trench, and setting off deep earthquakes and volcanic eruptions which in turn build mountains like those in the Aleutian Chain. When one plate grinds past another the crust is ripped in large faults. Pressure along these faults is released by thousands of small earthquakes.

Terranes - Alaska is like a giant puzzle with lots of different pieces that have come from lots of different places. Each piece is a big chunk of the earth's crust called a terrane. In fact, just about every piece of Alaska came from somewhere else. Where Southcentral Alaska is now there used to be a great ocean. During the time of the dinosaurs a big terrane was floating along the Pacific Plate near British Columbia. It eventually slid north and crashed into the rest of Alaska, displacing the ocean and forming the early Alaska Range.

Terrain - describes the way a landscape looks; swampy, mountainous etc. If you stood on top of the Brooks Range during the dinosaur days and looked around in a big circle, what would you see? To the west the mountains continue to rise, tall and jagged. Look north and a huge delta, cut with streams and bogs, stretches to the sea. South is an ocean ringed in volcanoes and to the east are more jagged mountains and low, rolling hills.

Beringia - a name given the land bridge and area around it that has often directly connected Asia and Alaska in the past.

North Slope - is the very top of Alaska; where the land meets the Arctic Ocean.

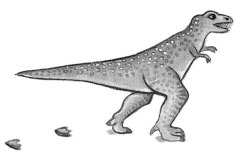

Mammoth Steppe - a huge area of Eurasia, including Alaska, that was alternately a dry, cold grassland during glacial periods, then warm with trees during the interglacial periods. The mammoth steppe was home to now extinct mammoths, bison, saiga antelope, camels, stag moose (moose with tremendous horns), mastodon, yaks, ground sloths, short-faced bears, lions, sabre-toothed cats and cheetahs.

Sloths - Sloths migrated north to Alaska from South America during an interglacial period. Camels came north from the mid-latitudes of the United States while mammoths, antelope and musk ox came east over the land bridge.

Ice ages - were times when glacial ice covered most of North America. During the most recent cold period there was a ice-free zone in the center of Alaska where many now extinct mammals lived. During the time of the mammoths the nights were very cold and clear. There was almost no precipitation. Temperature changes have caused many ice ages since the first one about 2.5 billion years ago; there have been 9 in just the last million years . . .

Mammals - Mammals are hairy, warm-blooded animals that nourish their young with milk from the mother. Many mammals that once lived here are now extinct. Even though Alaska is one of the last wilderness areas in the world where a variety of animals still flourish, there used to be many, many more creatures living here.

Plesiosaur - A large, long- necked, fish-eating reptile (not dinosaur) that lived in Alaska's oceans during the dinosaur days.

Reptiles - Scientists used to think that dinosaurs were reptiles like snakes or lizards. Now they aren't so sure. Reptiles can not regulate body temperature internally, so they must warm up in the sun in order to move around much. It would have been nearly impossible for a big dinosaur to ever get warm enough to move that way. Scientists now suspect that the earliest dino- saurs were cold-blooded, then later, carnivorous (meat-eating) dinosaurs evolved into warm- blooded creatures. Some of these same meat-eaters developed feathers and the ability to fly . . . today we call them birds.

What color were the dinosaurs?

We don't really know. It could be they were the colors of the land: green, brown or grey, so they would be camouflaged. Or perhaps they were red, pink or bright blue like peacocks or tropical fish.

Dragonflies-Dinosaurs ruled the earth for 150 million years but dragonflies hovered above the land long before even dinosaurs were around. They have lived on earth for at least 300 million years and probably followed a Beringia route from the Old to the New World.

THUNDERFEET

Lyrics and music © & ® Hobo Jim Varsos 1988
ASCAP

For Shaun from Dad, with love

The Troodon

It's true that a troodon likes to chew on
the bones of a hadrosaur.
But even a troodon has to move on
when he meets a tyannosaurus.
He's quick and smart enough to know
that he'd better go, go, go,
when he hears that mighty roar:
Rrrrrrrr I'mmm the great tyrannosaur!
It's true that a troodon likes to chew on
the bones of a hadrosaur.

Thunder Lizard

He's the tyrant lizard king tyrannosaurus.
He'll eat most anything, tyrannosaurus.
Can't you hear him singing in the chorus?
As he goes thunder, thunder, thunder, thunder,
thunder down the road.

The Counting Song

No horn, proteceratops,
one horn, monoclonius,
three horn, it's triceratops,
my favorite dinosaur.
Five horn, pentaceratops,
styracosaurus has many more.
Fighting's what they use them for.
WATCH OUT, Mr. Tyrannosaur.

Could You Care For a Short-faced Bear?

I have a song I'd like to share
because I am a short-faced bear.
The other creatures everywhere,
laugh and stare,
it's just not fair.
Could you care for a short-faced bear?
I roam the steppe from here to there,
searching for a friend so rare.
Sometimes I growl into the air,
and give myself an awful scare.
Oh could you care for a short-faced bear?

Prehistoric Pony

I want to ride on my prehistoric pony,
to the top of the growing Mt. Denali.
Together we will stand, looking over this great land,
as woolly mammoths graze down in the valley.
And I know as we pass by that sabre-toothed cat
we will fly just as fast as the wind.
We'll be riding so fine through the prehistoric times,
never to be seen again.

Let's have a Parade

Let's have a parade, a prehistoric parade.
And we'll dance around
with all the new friends we have made;
make dinosaur sounds, all through the night and the day.
Oh why don't we have a parade?